MW01535013

Decodable Stories
Kindergarten

Common Core Edition
Custom Edition

PEARSON

Glenview, Illinois • Boston, Massachusetts • Chandler, Arizona •
Upper Saddle River, New Jersey

Taken from:

Reader's & Writer's Notebook
Published by Pearson Education, Inc.
Upper Saddle River, New Jersey 07458

Pearson Learning Solutions, 501 Boylston Street, Suite 900, Boston, MA 02116
A Pearson Education Company
www.pearsoned.com

Printed in the United States of America

5 16

000200010271864929

RR

PEARSON   ISBN 10: 1-269-72821-0
ISBN 13: 978-1-269-72821-8

Unit 1: All Together Now

Unit 2: Look at Us!

Unit 3: Changes All Around Us

Unit 4: Let's Go Exploring

Unit 5: Going Places

Week 1: Max Takes the Train
  Jen and Will

Week 2: Mayday! Mayday!
  Max

Week 3: Trucks Roll!
  Fun for Jud

Week 4: The Little Engine That Could
  Jan and Gus

Week 5: On the Move!
  Val's Top

Week 6: This Is the Way We Go to School
  Run, Tim

Unit 6: Putting It Together

Week 1: Building with Dad
  Vin and the Bag

Week 2: Old MacDonald Had a Woodshop
  Spin the Top

Week 3: Building Beavers
  Jim and Kim

Week 4: Alistair and Kip's Great Adventure
  Gus and the Bug

Week 5: The House That Tony Lives In
  What Pets Do

Week 6: Ants and Their Nests
  What Can You Do?

I am bear.

© Pearson Education, Inc., K

Decodable Story *I Am!*
Letter Recognition *Aa, Bb, Cc, Dd, Ee*

I Am!

I am ant.

I am dog.

I am cat.

Am I iguana?

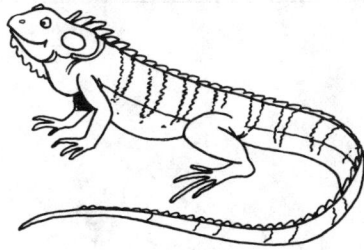

Am I monkey?

Am I kangaroo?

Name _____

Am I?

I am fish.

I am goose.

I am horse.

Little Me!

I am the little rabbit.

Am I the little seal?

Am I the little otter?

I am the little otter.

Decodable Story *Little Me!*
Letter Recognition *Oo, Pp, Qq, Rr, Ss*

Am I the little pig?

I am the little pig.

Am I the little quail?

I am the little quail.

Am I the little zebra?

Decodable Story *Am I Little?*
Letter Recognition *Tt, Uu, Vv, Ww, Xx, Yy, Zz*

Am I Little?

Am I the little turtle?

Am I the little van?

Am I the little

watermelon?

I walk to a little school.

4

Decodable Story *Little Mouse*
Target Skill /m/ Spelled *Mm*

Little Mouse

I am a little mouse.

1

I walk to a little school.

I am a little moose.

I walk to a table.

4

Tam!

I am Tam.

I am a turtle.

1

I walk to a tent.

I walk to a turkey.

I Have!

I have gum.

I have a cat.

The cat is little.

Decodable Story *I Have!*
Target Skill /a/ Spelled *Aa*

I have a rat.

The rat is little.

I have a ham.

The ham is little.

I have the sock.

Decodable Story *Sock Sack*
Target Skills /s/ Spelled *Ss*

Sock Sack

I have a sack.

The sock sack is little.

The sock is little.

I like to pat Pam.

Decodable Story *Pat the Cat*
Target Skill /p/ Spelled *Pp*

Pat the Cat

I like to pat my cat.

I pat my cat, Pam.

We pat Pam.

We like the caps.

Decodable Story *The Cap*
Target Skill /k/ Spelled *Cc*

The Cap

I have a cap.

The cap is my cap.

I like my cap.

He is a little pig.

Decodable Story *Tim the Pig*
Target Skill /i/ Spelled *Ii*

Tim the Pig

Tim the pig is little.

Tim the pig can tap it.

Tim the pig can pat it.

Sit, pat, sip.

Decodable Story *Sam, Sit!*
Target Skill /i/ Spelled *Ii*

Sam, Sit!

Sam, sit.

Sam, pat.

Sam, sip.

Nat sat.

Nan sat with Nat.

Nan and Nat

I am Nan.

I am Nat.

We have nets.

Nan is with Nat.

Nat can nab with a net.

Nat nabs with the net.

Nan nabs with the net.

Rin ran to Rip.

Rip ran.

© Pearson Education, Inc., K

Rin the Rat

Rin is a rat.

She is a little rat.

Rin likes to tap.

She can tap.

Rip ran to Rin.

He is with Rin.

Pit ran to the dish.

Pit did.

4

Pit Did!

Pit can see the duck.

Pit ran with the duck.

Pit did.

1

Pit can see the doll.

Pit ran to the doll.

Pit can look at the door.

Pit ran to the door.

Pit did.

I see a fin for me.

Look at the fin.

For Me!

I see a fan for me.

Look at the fan.

I see a fox for me.

Look at the little fox.

I see a fish for me.

Look at the little fish.

Little Rob is not sad.

Little Rob can have
the top.

© Pearson Education, Inc., K

Little Rob

Little Rob is sad.

He is little.

Little Rob is on a mat.

He is sad.

Little Rob can see a top.

Can he have the top?

It is not on the rat.

It is in the pot.

A Cap for Tom

Tom can have a cap.

Is the cap on Tom?

The cap is not on Tom.
See the cap.

The cap is not on Tom.
It is on the rat.

I like my hat.

Do you like my hat?

4

Decodable Story *I Have!*
Target Skill /h/ Spelled *Hh*

I Have!

I have a hat.

The hat is little.

That is my hat.

1

The hat is on me.

It is my little hat.

Do you have a little hat?

I can hop with the hat.

I can hit with the hat.

Lad can hop on the lid.

I can do that.

Are we on the lid?

4

Decodable Story *Lad and Me*
Target Skill /l/ Spelled *Ll*

Lad and Me

Lad is my cat.

Lad is little.

Do you like Lad?

4 I

I like Lad.

Lad can sit in my lap.

Lad can sit a lot.

Lad can hop.

Lad can hop a lot.

I can do that.

I can tap.

Tap is like trap.

Do you see one trap?

4

Decodable Story *My Words*
Target Skill Consonant Blends

My Words

I have one cap.

Cap is like clap.

Can you clap?

1

I see one cab.

Cab is like crab.

Can you see three?

I can see one pot.

Pot is like spot.

Do you see two?

Can you see four frogs?

Lin and Hap can see
five frogs.

Decodable Story *How Many?*
Target Skill /g/ Spelled *Gg*

How Many?

Lin and Hap can see
one dog.

Lin and Hap can see
two kids.

Lin and Hap can see
three pigs.

ten hens

ten bells

ten pens

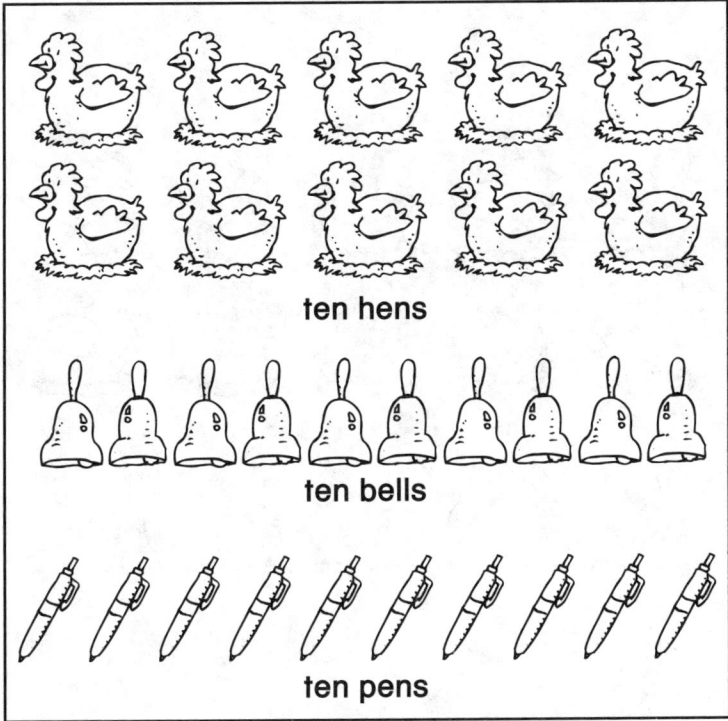

I see ten, ten, ten!

© Pearson Education, Inc., K

Decodable Story *Ten, Ten, Ten!*
Target Skill /e/ Spelled *Ee*

Ten, Ten, Ten!

I have a pet hen.

Do you see my hen?

I can see ten.

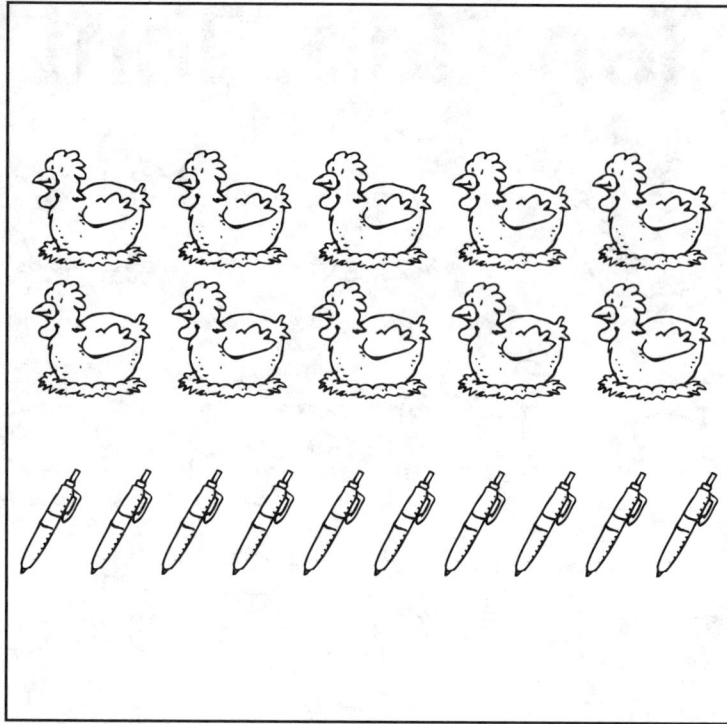

I have a fat pen.

Do you see my pen?

I can see ten.

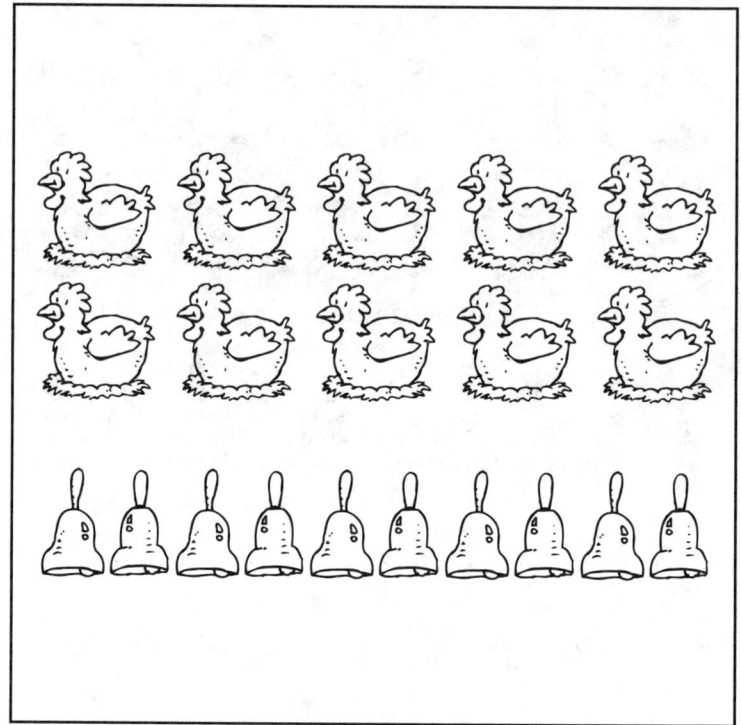

I have a red bell.

Do you see my bell?

I can see ten.

You can see the tent.

You can see the nest.

I have a pet.

Decodable Story *Ted and the Pet*
Target Skill /e/ Spelled *Ee*

Ted and the Pet

I am Ted.

I have a pet.

My pet is big.

I met my pet here.

My pet is in the tent.

It is a big tent.

My pet can go to the tent.

My pet has a nest in
the tent.

It is a big nest.

You can get on the big, blue jet.

You can go with Jen and Will.

Decodable Story *Jen and Will*
Target Skill /j/ Spelled *Jj*, /w/ Spelled *Ww*

Jen and Will

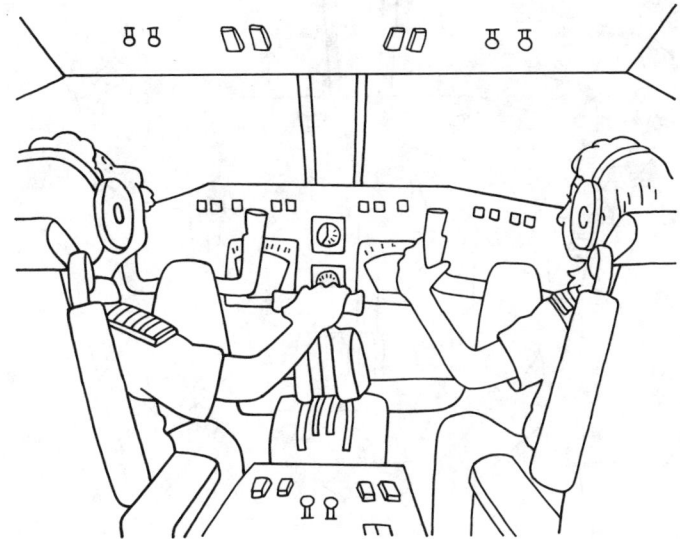

Jen and Will get on the jet.

It is a big, blue jet.

Jen and Will have jobs
on the jet.

Jen and Will like the jobs.

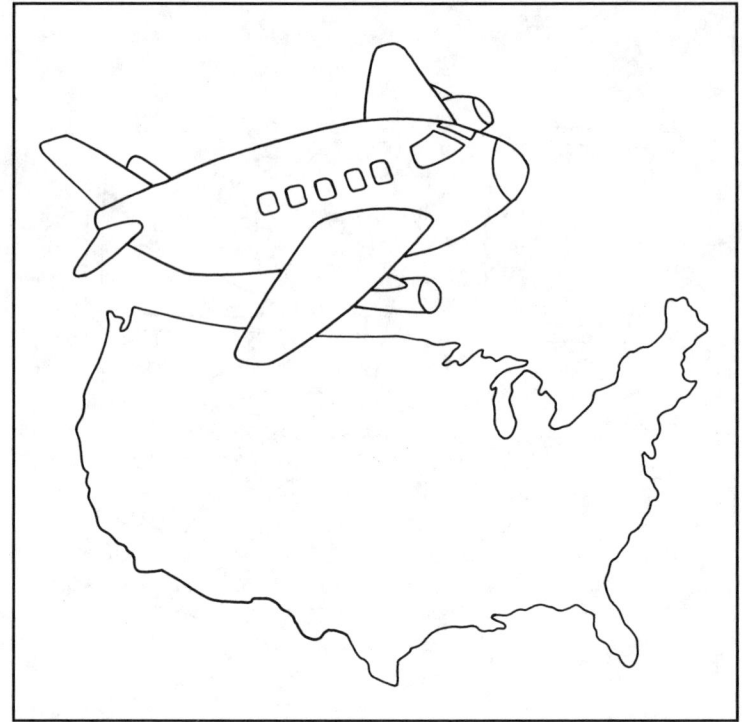

Jen and Will get the jet
to go.

They can see you.

Max can see his pal Rex.

Max and Rex can mix
yellow and red.

Decodable Story *Max*
Target Skill /ks/ Spelled *Xx*

Max

Max is six.

He hid in a box.

He hid from his mom.

Max can look like a fox.

He has four legs.

Max can mix blue and green.

It is an ox.

Jud ran to his pals.

Jud said, "Let us go in!

We will have fun!"

Decodable Story *Fun for Jud*
Target Skill /u/ Spelled *Uu*

Fun for Jud

The sun was hot.

Jud got up from bed.

Jud has to have a plan.

What can he do for fun?

Jud will see his pals.

What will they do for fun?

Jan and Gus are on
the rug.

Jan and Gus are pals.

4

© Pearson Education, Inc., K

Decodable Story *Jan and Gus*
Target Skill /u/ Spelled *Uu*

Jan and Gus

Jan and Gus are pals.

They like to have fun.

Jan and Gus like the sun.

They like to hum on the bus.

Jan and Gus see a bug.

They run in the mud.

He will zap the tag.

Val has got the red top.

Decodable Story *Val's Top*
Target Skill /v/ Spelled *Vv*, /z/ Spelled *Zz*

Val's Top

Val and Mom come in a van.

They will go to look for a top.

Val and Mom see a top.

They can zip it up.

The top is red.

Val and Mom like the top.

Tim ran to the end.

Tim had a rest.

4

Decodable Story *Run, Tim*
Target Skill /y/ Spelled *Yy*, /kw/ Spelled *Qq*

Run, Tim

Tim ran past his sis.

She said,

"You can not quit yet."

1

Tim ran up a hill.

His dad said,

"You can not quit yet."

2

Tim ran and ran.

His mom said,

"You can not quit yet."

3

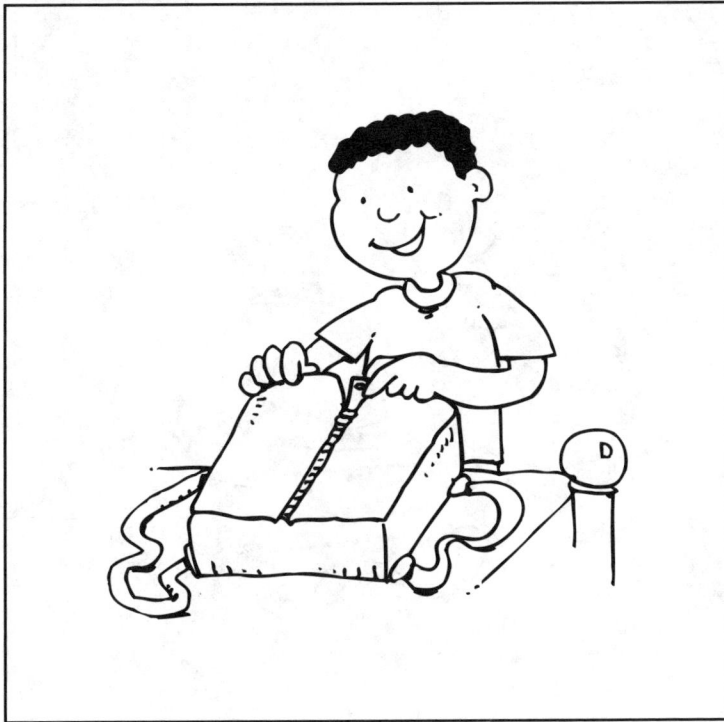

Vin will zip the bag.

He and the bag will go
on a trip.

4

Vin and the Bag

Vin had a bag.

The bag is a big bag.

1

He got one big can.

He got one little net.

He got one little kit.

He got one big rag.

Dad will spin the top.

Dad can spin it.

Dad can get the top
to spin.

4

Spin the Top

Bob got a top.

Bob will spin the top.

1

The top will not spin.

The top will not go.

Help! Help!

Help me spin the top.

It will not spin.

Help! Help!

The hen had little ones.

Jim and Kim have lots of little hens.

Jim and Kim

Jim and Kim had a pet.

They had a pet hen.

The hen was in a pen.

Jim had fun with the pet hen.

Jim fed the hen.

Kim had fun with the pet hen.

Kim got a nest for the hen.

Gus grabs the bug.

Gus lets the bug go.

© Pearson Education, Inc., K

Name _____

Gus and the Bug

Gus will hug his mom.

Gus gets on the bus.

Gus sat with his pal Wes.

The sun was hot.

A bug got on the bus.

It sat with Gus and Wes.

Sam is a cat.

Sam will sit in a lap.

He will nap.

What Pets Do

Peg is a dog.

She will tug.

She will dig.

Hal is a pet pig.

He will run in his pen.

He will go in the mud.

2

Tad is a pet frog.

He will hop.

He will swim.

3

I am Jen.

I can hang from my legs.

What can you do?

Decodable Story *What Can You Do?*
Target Skill Review

Name _____

What Can You Do?

Here is Ned.

Ned can run fast.

Ned can run and run.

Look at Ken.

He fed the big dog.

He fed the little dogs.

2

See Kim jump.

She can go from me to you.

She can jump from here
to here.

3